1SELF

REINVENT YOURSELF
TO RISE FROM ANY CRISIS

par LINKED IN AND TOWN HALL ACHIEVER OF THE YEAR
NOMINÉ ENTREPRENEUR DE L'ANNÉE ERNST & YOUNG
GRAND HOMMAGE À LYS DIVERSITÉ
WORLD TOP100 DOCTORS

Dr. BAK NGUYEN, DMD

TO EVERYONE LOOKING AHEAD IN CHALLENGING TIMES,
IT STARTS WITH HOPE, IT GROWS WITH RESILIENCE
AND ONCE IT STARTED, IT NEVER STOPS.

by Dr. BAK NGUYEN

Copyright © 2021 Dr. BAK NGUYEN

All rights reserved.

ISBN: 978-1-989536-55-1

ABOUT THE AUTHORS

From Canada, **Dr. BAK NGUYEN**, Nominee Ernst and Young Entrepreneur of the year, Grand Homage Lys DIVERSITY, LinkedIn & TownHall Achiever of the year and TOP 100 Doctors 2021. Dr Bak is a cosmetic dentist, CEO and founder of Mdex & Co. His company is revolutionizing the dental field. Speaker and motivator, he wrote 72 books over 36 months accumulating many world records (to be officialized). His books are covering:

- **ENTREPRENEURSHIP**
- **LEADERSHIP**
- **QUEST OF IDENTITY**
- **DENTISTRY AND MEDICINE**
- **PARENTING**
- **CHILDREN BOOKS**
- **PHILOSOPHY**

In 2003, he founded Mdex, a dental company upon which in 2018, he launched the most ambitious private endeavour to reform the dental industry, Canada wide. Philosopher, he has close to his heart the quest of happiness of the people surrounding him, patients and colleagues alike. In 2020, he launched an International collaborative initiative named **THE ALPHAS** to share knowledge and for Entrepreneurs and Doctors to thrive through the Greatest Pandemic and Economic depression of our time.

In 2016, he co-found with Tranie Vo, Emotive World Incorporated, a tech research company to use technology to empower happiness and sharing. U.A.X. the ultimate audio experience is the landmark project on which the team is advancing, utilizing the technics of the movie industry and the advancement in ARTIFICIAL INTELLIGENCE to save the book industry and to upgrade the continuing education space.

These projects have allowed Dr Nguyen to attract interests from the international and diplomatic community and he is now the center of a global discussion in the wellbeing and the future of the health profession. It is in that matter that he shares his thoughts and encourages the health community to share their own stories.

"It's not worth it go through it alone! Together, we stand, alone, we fall."

Motivational speaker and serial entrepreneur, philosopher and author, from his own words, Dr Nguyen describes himself as a dentist by circumstances, an entrepreneur by nature and a communicator by passion.

He also holds recognitions from the Canadian Parliament and the Canadian Senate.

1SELF
REINVENT YOURSELF
TO RISE FROM ANY CRISIS

by Dr. BAK NGUYEN

INTRODUCTION
BY Dr BAK NGUYEN

THE MAP
CHAPTER 1 - Dr. BAK NGUYEN

THE RISE
CHAPTER 2 - Dr. BAK NGUYEN

THE TIME IS NOW
CHAPTER 3 - Dr. BAK NGUYEN

THE FORGE
CHAPTER 4 - Dr. BAK NGUYEN

SMALL WINS ARE HUGE
CHAPTER 5 - Dr. BAK NGUYEN

THE CATERPILLAR EFFECT
CHAPTER 6 - Dr. BAK NGUYEN

OVERACHIEVING
CHAPTER 7 - Dr. BAK NGUYEN

JEALOUSY
CHAPTER 8 - Dr. BAK NGUYEN

CONCLUSION
BY Dr BAK NGUYEN

INTRODUCTION
by Dr. BAK NGUYEN

I just published my 77th book, **POWERPLAY, HOW TO BUILD THE PERFECT TEAM**. Apple Books, Amazon, and Kindle are now distributing it.

You see, I was looking for a way to flush down 2020 down the toilets and to start fresh 2021. For a month, I was looking for that symbolic. I asked around, but no one came back to me with a viral answer.

The morning of December 31st, I woke up with a crazy idea, to flush down 2020 with a world record, my newest book. That morning, I posted on my social wall the following: "My question is, will I finish the year with a world record or will I start the new year with one?"

For some, as usual, that was me bragging. They missed the whole point. That was me challenging myself, once more to reinvent myself, to rewrite the future.

> "To reinvent ourselves is to rewrite the future."
> Dr. Bak Nguyen

But now, I just invented a new title to write, out of the blue, and right after the writing of **THE RISE OF THE UNICORN 2** that will be co-written with Dr. Jean De Serres. Jean will be starting soon, I have completed my 8 chapters of that book.

I also started and finished my 77th book, a new series for kids, **THE VACCINE, A TALE OF SPIES AND ALIENS**, co-written with my 10-year-old son, William Bak. That last one promises to be huge since it is breaking down the science behind the vaccine, in words that will keep the interest of kids.

The momentum started as I wrote down the first words. I finished that book within 3 hours, maybe 4. Then, I asked for a favor from a friend. The manuscript will be medically reviewed by the former CEO of Hema Quebec, the equivalent of the Red Cross! Thank you Jean!

I did not realize how huge and impactful that project was. Then, I got my team together to have the imagery done by a great artist. Meeting with my executive team, my producers agreed on the merits of this project and are now packaging it to become our entrance to NETFLIX with a special animated documentary. We still have to pitch NETFLIX and to sell them the idea!

In the meantime, William and I are getting down to write the French version of **THE VACCINE**, completing my 79th book. Yup, every time that I have to work twice, it is another book to my count! Do you have any idea our hard it is for me to work a second time on the same subject?

And to keep the vibe moving forward, we are planning (Dr. Bak's style and pace) to produce the **U.A.X** version (audio-movie) of **THE VACCINE**, maybe in more than one language.

So while in the middle of that comfortable storm of creativity, I had the crazy idea to start yet another book and to have it complete with less than 2 days, from beginning to delivering. Oh, haven't I told you that we are now also producing in parallel, the audio version of my books and have them available as combo paperback - audiobook?

Well, it is done. As of this morning, **POWERPLAY** is live on all the major outlets, I am just waiting for it arrival at Barnes and Noble to say: "Mission Accomplished!" I would have successfully started the new year with one world record, or two…

Well, I am pretty relieved to know that I haven't lost my touch since I haven't written much last fall, after my last stream of world records leading me to write 72 books within 36 months. I haven't lost my momentum.

That being said, this is book #80. What about book #74? Well, 0074 is titled **COVIDCONOMICS.** It might take 9-10 months to write since it will be a world phenomenon and collaboration. The dateline is August 2021 so it can be part of my next set of world records.

So what is coming next after 72 books over 36 months? 96 books over 48 months? I told you that I liked the rounded numbers, why not make it 100 books over 4 years? I liked the numbers and the change in wording.

100 books?! But that will be 4 more on top of the usual 2 books a month. And I wrote only 1 book within the last 3 months! I went through the numbers and that will mean that I will have 21 books to write within the next 8 months. That's an average of 2.3 books a month!

Can I do that? To be honest, I don't know. This is overwhelming. Sure, the last time, I wrote a book every 8 days on average for 8 weeks to reach 72 books within 36 months. My best was 30 hours, writing **EMPOWERMENT**. I could have done that one in less than 24 hours but I decided to nap twice!

The problem isn't the writing, but the motivation and the subjects. Can I find more and more subjects to write about that I master and have any interest in? Can I keep my focus on writing books while the toll of the media had cut by more than half my available creativity and time?

The **ALPHASHOW**, the **ALPHACLASS**, the **U.A.X.**, and coming soon, the NETFLIX productions are all taking so much of my time. Keep in mind that I am not only writing but editing and publishing these books to most of the known channels: print, ebook, audiobooks (**U.A.X.**).

As I told my friend and co-author (of my 63rd book, **AFTERMATH**) Dr. Eric Lacoste, I want to find out where is the limit? How far can I go, writing about Life, about us, and about Hope?

To keep the fun in the game, I have developed the **APOLLO** protocol to help me write even faster. The **APOLLO** protocol allows the writing of a book within 24 hours, going through a scripted interview. The process is proven and very efficient, but something keeps pushing me to write old style, from my laptop.

> *"To write is to meditate,
> only with consequences."*
> Dr. Bak Nguyen

That's why I like to write because it has become my *ME* time. Well, I don't know about you, but I can't meditate while talking, and the **APOLLO** protocol is all about talking. Writing is all about feeling and listening to our inner voice.

So this book will be written from my reflections and meditation, old style. I guess I will use the **APOLLO** protocol as I am running out of inspiration and looking for a fun way to keep my interest.

So 21? That's a lot of books and even more words. I should be close to 1.3 million words written as I am writing these exact words.

> "This has become a number's game,
> one with many words."
> Dr. Bak Nguyen

What has changed is that I am today working on multiple books at the same time. This is so confusing, but since **COVIDCONOMICS** will take 9 months, I can't afford to wait for that one to be over before starting a new one. In pipeline, **KISS ORTHODONTICS** is waiting with co-author, Dr. Ouellette.

To be able to keep writing and sharing, I must live, I must learn and I must be able to adapt. And that's the main subject bringing us together today, to be able to keep moving forward.

1SELF is about being authentic to share. **1SELF** is about being open at Life to keep learning, to keep feeling. **1SELF** is about beating our own personal best, to look back saying that I went so far since…

> "Once a mind reached a higher level of energy,
> it can simply not go back to its previous level."
> Albert Einstein

How about using the last level as a stepping stone to reach higher and higher? How about using today as a step for tomorrow, and tomorrow as a step for the day after tomorrow? Sounds simple enough? It can only be achieved with the right mindset, the **right balance** of **confidence, humility**, and **innocence**.

CONFIDENCE since to move forward faster and further, one must have the arrogance to not care for others' opinions. Seek and listen to experiences, not opinions.

The difference lays in action, as experience is the story of actions and decisions, wherever the result; while *opinion is the poem of fear and hypothesis at best*. I learn that one from RON KLEIN, one of the great American modern innovators.

HUMILITY since our best victory will only be useful as stepping stones for tomorrow. Not just to us, but to all those who will be following. Everyone will be stepping on those victories we once held dear.

If we keep the medals on the wall, we are serving the medals and the past. If we use them as stepping stones, they are paving the way to our next journey. **HUMILITY** will assure the continuation of your journey, even if you thought that there is nothing left for you to explore or to learn.

> "HUMILITY is the KEYSTONE to RELEVANCY."
> Dr. Bak Nguyen

To never become a *"HAS BEEN"*, to never lose momentum, to keep the rise. **HUMILITY** is the key to fun and eternal youth.

And **INNOCENCE** since to keep moving forward with fun, one must have the hope that there is more, that there is better ahead. That ability to experience something for the first time, time and time over, is what keeps our hearts young and adventurous.

A little earlier, I was talking about motivation. Well, perpetual motivation can be found in INNOCENCE.

To be faster than EVOLUTION, to keep our RELEVANCY and FUN thanks to CONFIDENCE, HUMILITY, and INNOCENCE, that's the journey ahead. That's the promise of **1SELF**.

If **COVIDCONOMICS** is about the ongoing changes and shifts in our society, **1SELF** is about helping you to adapt, to leverage, and to surf the changes and shifts to rise from surviving to thriving.

This is **1SELF,** reinvent yourself from any crisis.

To be faster than EVOLUTION,
To keep our RELEVANCY and FUN
Thanks to CONFIDENCE,
HUMILITY and INNOCENCE,

That's the journey ahead.
That's the promise of **1SELF**.

Dr. BAK NGUYEN

CHAPTER 1
THE MAP

by Dr. BAK NGUYEN

I was wondering how to start this book, this 80th book. How about jazzing it up a little bit. Isn't that the spirit, to reinvent ourselves? If you are holding this book today, you feel it in you that you must do something new, something different. You feel it inside that you are ready for a change?

That gut feeling that you are experiencing is your inner voice, your instincts voicing up. Embracing change, that can be exhilarating to some, but to most, it is the biggest source of anxiety and stress.

So how can you explain that you feel the desire to change from inside, while most of our lives, we've been trying to avoid anxiety and stress? How does that even make sense? From personal experience, I can tell you that it isn't the desire for change that you are experimenting, but the desire to reveal… your true self.

Only your true nature can give you that intense urge to be different. Different from what? Different from who you are today. Not everyone is looking for their true self at the same time, but sooner or later, we all are. This is called the **Question of Identity**.

By **Question of Identity**, I do not mean your name, last name nor job career. I meant your choices and your values. No, that is not a mistake, choices first and values after.

This should surprise many of you. Common wisdom will tell us that we are making our choices based upon our values. So values have to come first, right? Are we making our choices from our values, or are we making our choices based on the values that our surroundings have given us? And to follow that flow, to embrace the values of the Collective, was our choice, in the first place.

> "Choice first, values come after."
> Dr. Bak Nguyen

Even those who were never fully aware of that choice, made one: to close their eyes and to follow. Our name is given to us. Our last name, we have inherited it even before our birth.

And our profession and careers? To most, we were given the choice between what was in the right hand and what was in the other right hand. Those are our education system and the peer pressure of our family and cycle of friends. That's what we call social status.

And we adapted, we moved with it. We even successfully managed to be good at what we do, from our choices by default. That's great! And it will last for a moment.

Within the first few years, it was about the pressure to fit in and to prove ourselves worthy. Then, the small rewards and recognitions kept us on track to perform. That performance of ours made us who we are until we feel that urge for change within our guts.

All of us will feel that calling, sooner or later. It will be very unsettling and will re-question everything that we chose by default, following **Conformity**, not our Nature.

That's the personal **Quest of Identity** that all of us will walk, sooner or later. In our modern society, we have another word to label it, some are calling it the **Midlife Crisis**! Whatever the label, it all boils down to the re-questioning of our values and the remaking or confirmation of most of our choices.

This is what happened in the flow of Life as we are growing and enjoying freedom and abundance. Abraham Maslow, the famous American psychologist dedicated part of his professional life to describe and to map the phenomenon. He summarized the journey with the Pyramid of Maslow.

SELF-ACTUALIZATION
ESTEEM
LOVE/BELONGING
SAFETY
PHYSIOLOGICAL NEEDS

THE PYRAMID OF ABRAHAM MASLOW

At the base of the pyramid are the **PHYSIOLOGICAL NEEDS**, to eat, to sleep, etc. Then, comes the second layer, **SAFETY**, to shelter, to reproduce, looking for stability. At the middle of the pyramid are **LOVE** and **BELONGING**. Then, the need for **ESTEEM** and, at the top of the pyramid is **SELF-ACTUALIZATION**, the need for a purpose.

The **Quest of Identity** level is at the **ESTEEM** and **SELF-ACTUALIZATION** levels, once our basic needs and sense of belonging have been secured.

Following that logic, sooner or later, we are all moving up the ladders of Life, of our personal evolution, unless someone is pressing on the **RESET BUTTON**.

By **RESET BUTTON**, war, illness, immigration are part of those stimuli setting us back at the base of the pyramid and having us climb back the ladder, once again.

> "Any crisis has the potential to be a RESET BUTTON, if not total, at least partial."
> Dr. Bak Nguyen

And this brings us to the **CRISIS** part of this journey. I am writing these lines in the midst of the COVID war. At the time of this writing, we are not on the winning side. For now almost a year, we have been in **RESET** mode, all of us.

What are we doing in **RESET** mode? What is happening? How are we feeling? That insecurity that we are bathing in daily, that's not just COVID, that's not just grief or our frustration towards the authorities, that's also the **RESETTING** of our values.

You see, there is a universal law of nature that will have all of us evolve to rebecome what we were, at our core, from our creation. These values forced into us, these choices by default, all these times that we were not courageous enough to listen to our inner voice, all of that will slowly melt and fade away.

In other words, unless you have freely chosen specific values, at your **RESET POINT**, those values will disappear, unless you are now freely devoting yourself to them. I am saying devoting, because what is a value but a mindset and set of rules that will restrict your liberty and freedom of choices?

> "Values are boundaries.
> Nothing less and nothing more."
> Dr. Bak Nguyen

The **RESET BUTTON** is propelling us out of our own system of belief for a little while, allowing us a moment of freedom and the opportunity of a perspective of our lives and choices. Then, we will have to fit back in, but with that **FEELING OF FREEDOM** and that **AWARENESS OF CHOICES**.

And this is what we are doing now, all at the same time, we are fitting back in the system, after a forced and abrupt interruption of our flow. Some will say that it is a blessing. Some others will say that it was an unneeded burden.

Well, I told you that sooner or later, we all walk that walk. The problem here is that everyone is resetting at the same time, leaving very few people steady to serve as guidance points.

> "By definition, all systems are moving.
> Their stability is coming from the continuation
> of their dynamic."
> Dr. Bak Nguyen

And without dynamic, at the standstill point, the balance is lost and a new dynamic will emerge. This is where we are, at the **emergence** of the **new dynamic**.

Our reflexes will push us to try to resume as we were. But very soon, we will take notice that the coming back to where we were, a minute ago, is a long process back up to the hill, most of the time, not even the top. This is without considering that everyone else is also lining up to climb back that hill!

And because it happened so fast, the feelings of abundance and of freedom were still very present in our hearts. We just gain the gift of time, for a little while.

Following the Pyramid of Maslow, this is where we are situated, at the mid-point of the Pyramid, floating at **BELONGING**. Our choices are either to look up, at **ESTEEM** or to look down at **SECURITY**. For now, we are all belonging to the mass of the people fallen from the hill.

And whatever choice you will be making now will define you for the next years ahead, maybe decades. Somehow, that, we all know.

> "It is always time to change,
> but somehow, it is never the right timing."
> Dr. Bak Nguyen

Well, long ago, I've learnt to not judge anyone. I empower those I can and I keep walking my own path. If you are looking down and looking to reach **SAFETY**, you know the way. The line starts at the bottom of the hill. I wish you luck and thank you for your contribution to the stability of our systems.

For those of you who are looking up, looking for **ESTEEM** and **PURPOSE**, you, I understand and can help. That urge of yours to be more, to be better, that I can help. The way up is not a safe nor a known one, but it is one with less resistance and friction than the lower layers of the pyramid, of the hill.

This is exactly as the laws of Physic, the force of Gravity grounding us down diminishes as we are climbing the mountain.

> "Moving up, the air might be scarcer, but in exchange, you gain horizon and perspective, leading you to clarity."
> Dr. Bak Nguyen

And this is our journey ahead, together. As we are moving up, we are skipping the lines at the bottom of the hill. But as we are moving up, we will also need to adapt to the new air ratio and to preserve our breath.

Every time that we will raise up our heads to see, the horizon will be beautiful and grandiose, always expanding. But we won't have much air to waste… so losing our breath, we might never make it to the next level, left alone, the top.

This is **1SELF**, reinvent yourself from any crisis.

To be faster than EVOLUTION,
To keep our RELEVANCY and FUN
Thanks to CONFIDENCE,
HUMILITY and INNOCENCE,

That's the journey ahead.
That's the promise of **1SELF**.

Dr. BAK NGUYE

CHAPTER 2
T H E   R I S E

by Dr. BAK NGUYEN

The key importance of the previous chapter is **DYNAMIC**. Why is it that we are all falling from the Hill as we stood still? Because we are falling out of the flow. And this is the basis of Life, a flow.

So the first lie to clear our minds of is that nothing stands still. Standing still in appearance is, in fact, balancing the forces to give the illusion and the impression of not moving.

In truth, standing still, you are dedicating your life force to balance all the variation of energy, of flow, of events, absorbing and compensating. That was not free, it was exhausting!

But we are resilient, all of us. Even those with fewer ambitions, will all managed to find a way to *"standstill"* and devoted their Lifeforce to that purpose.

That being said, what happened in the COVID war, in confinement? Well, we've been asked to stay home and to stop our daily lives as we know-how. And then, we fell. We just fell. You can be in denial, you can explain it, but you all felt its effect, falling down.

Right before the fall, because the stop was so abrupt, pretty unreal to most, we were expelled from our standing still point and we were all projected into the horizon. Before the **law of Gravity** could catch up, we had our few stolen moments, floating freely in space.

This is what you felt getting up in the morning and reliving the same day over and over again within the first confinement. That's when you felt when time was looping. You felt lost, we all were. You felt weird, we all did. And then, the bubble burst and the **law of Gravity** reclaimed its power over all of its subjects.

Well, facing such force of nature, all one can do is it to submit. Or is there an alternative? The laws of Nature and its forces are all based on balance, cause and effect, actions, and consequences. So what would be the effect and consequences of the law of Gravity?

Well, one can obey and fall. Or one can present a force of equal power and float. Or one can present an even more powerful force to rise above.

> "The Universe is a dynamic balancing the forces. You have to decide what you are in that dynamic, a force, or an effect."
> Dr. Bak Nguyen

If you are reading these lines, if you are holding this book and that you keep reading, I think that we can assume that you have found your **WHY**, the reason to stop being an effect, and to endure the consequences of the forces surrounding you.

In other words, you have awoken and are now ready to walk your quest of Identity and, eventually your legend. If you are wondering about those quests, I will refer you to my 4th book, **IDENTITY, The Anthology of Quests**.

This journey, **1SELF**, is more about how to rise and to become a force balancing with Gravity. Be careful of the wording and intention, the first mistake to avoid is to confront the laws of Nature, opposing it with what we are. Trust me, you won't last long, no one will.

But to every law in Nature, there is another one, counter-balancing it. At first sight, they might be opposing, even contradictory, but with perspective, one was taking over where the other ends. And if you can feel that reality, eventually, you might understand it, and more importantly, leverage it.

In other words, I am not telling you to rebel and to oppose any of the realities that you know. I am telling you to create a new one. By creating a new reality, the only friction you might have is your own mind, your doubts. At least for a while, that reality was solely in your heart and your head, and no one else knew about it.

Nurture that reality and experience its dynamic, laws, and effects. If you believe, you will grow that reality of yours from projection into dynamic. Because the more you believe, the more you live in it. Now, it has become an alternate reality, one you have to balance with the other realities you were bathing in.

I know, all of those might sound quite abstract, but for those who are experiencing it, it is as true and real as breathing, as looking outside, as taking a walk.

> "Give it a try to feel,
> to understand."
> Dr. Bak Nguyen

What is your vision, what is that alternate reality of yours, it is for you to decide. But once free from all exterior influences and forces, whatever is left is your profound desires and path to your own happiness.

This is higher than Self-love, it is Esteem, leading to Confidence. Coming back to the pyramid of Maslow, you are leaving the middle of the pyramid to climb a step higher, to reach **ESTEEM**. Well, that desire of yours since it is natural will gain the respect of Gravity.

As result, where you thought you would be crushed facing an immense force of Nature, you will rise instead. Because you were in tune, in harmony with another primal frequency of Nature, your own evolution and awakening.

This is how men and women have distinguished themselves throughout History. To us, reading and listening about it, they are heroes fighting monsters and riding the storm while in truth, they were walking through the **FOG** until it thinners and fades to leave the place for light to shine.

There were not opposing Nature, laws, or any Gods, there were walking their path of Life. Opposing Nature, they will have never made it back since how can one opposes something that he or she is a part of? Playing that game is a lose - lose scenario.

No, they walked their path, one step after the next, and they found their path as if it was always intended to be walked. I am sure that this is not the first time that you are hearing such rhetoric and theme. Ask yourself why the theme is a familiar one, and yet, why it is so far from your reality?

Actually, there is no lie here, both realities are true. The fight, the storm, and the battle on one side. On the other, the walk, the enlightenment, the liberation. Well, having walked that path myself, here is what I can tell you:

The Storm is our attachments
And the conflicted emotions about letting go
The Monsters and Demons were no other than our Fear
And the traitors within our ranks
Were often Doubts and Pride

That's the **walk of Identity** that all will walk, sooner or later. The lies are the ones that we accepted and feed ourselves with daily. The pain is our refusal to let go of the past, ugly and beautiful. The real drama here is to be chained to the past.

That will suffocate you and creates its own clouds and limits, defining its own reality and laws. Those are the ones you will be fighting, rising up, not the laws of Nature.

In that sense, Nature is very kind and patient since it has allowed everything to be under the sun. We made the clouds and the rest.

So, I guess, what I am telling you here is that walking your path and rising is Natural and you will have the support of Nature, at least, you will not be opposing any forces greater than yourself.

That being said, it won't be a walk in the park. To most of us, we have been living in a very rigid reality, one of safety, one of security, and one aiming for perfection. Each of those has its own sets of rules, laws, even gravity. To those, we all obeyed. It is that fight that will be hard.

To fight an enemy, as frightened as it can be, is always easier than to face a demon with a friendly face, one you trust and love. Yes, those demons have the face of your past, of those you love, and it is the most frightened, it will have your face in the final confrontation. Well, those are fears and doubts.

The demons may have your face, but not your heart, that's the only thing that you alone possess and decide to give away to whom you love. And the magic of a heart is that once given, can be given again and again with more intensity.

To understand that concept, ask any parents how do they love their kids. Each relationship is unique and different, but never lesser because one took more love, leaving nothing less for the others.

> "Attention is not love, as attention can only be divided, love can be multiplied."
> Dr. Bak Nguyen

So your attention was the center of Gravity of your whole reality and its balance. Whatever has your attention will be real and will take more importance on your scale, in your truth. And the fight for your attention is one with no mercy.

Having walked through the storm myself, I will tell you that to win that fight, you need allies and tools. For those, you have to open your eyes and your heart to find on your way. I can tell you that they are not easy to find, but once you have gained clarity opening your heart, when you find them, you know they are meant for you.

These tools, armor, swords, shield, they will serve you for a while and then, you will have to leave them behind to keep walking your path without unnecessary burden.

> "What is an asset today may become your biggest liability tomorrow."
> Dr. Bak Nguyen

And that is why you do not want to get attached. Be gracious, be grateful, but not attached since that is what creating the **FOG** in the first place.

Learn to let go. To let go of your successes, to let go of your failures, to let go of your hate; to especially let go of those you love, unless you want to see their faces as your demons and your face as theirs.

We are meant to come together and to share, for a moment. That moment can be brief, that moment can be of several years, when there is attraction, the connection will live for another day.

Attraction is based on your attention and devotion. Well, eventually, since Attention cannot be multiplied, you will need to move on, to focus your attention on the next ladder of your own evolution.

No one can be forever 21, and even if you've found a way to trick the system, looking 21 for longer, you are not feeling 21. The *vampire wisdom* in our folklore covers that theme very well.

If you wanted to live forever, start with the first part of the desire: to live! And to live, you will have to try, to taste, and to be changed by what you tasted and touched. Those are the first steps.

Then, if you are genuine and are truly living your evolution, you will see the ripple effect of your presence on your surrounding. If what you tasted and touched changed you, you are also changing the perspective of what you touched and of those tasting you. It is in that sense that your essence may prevail and last forever.

I said to change their perspectives, not themselves. And this is a big difference. Unlike what religion has preached for so long, you do not want to convert anyone. You are living your lives and passing through.

Since you have your own walk to pursue, you are leaving them with inspiration and perspective, an alternative, not laws and set of rules to follow.

By doing so, you will move on lighter and happier. Doing so, they will remember you as an ally and a kind guide. And it will all boil down to what are they devoting their attention to. The same logic goes for you, but since you are looking to rise, your attention is on your path, ahead.

You wanted to know how to reinvent yourself and to rise? I showed you the primal laws and the map. I also warned you about the demons, the monsters, and the storm ahead.

I told you about the tools and the leverage. And I gave you the hope that the walk isn't as bad as it looks. Once inside the Storm, there is the **FOG**, but no real danger. Once inside the **FOG**, there are demons. The hardest demons are the ones with familiar faces.

Are you ready to rise? I showed you how, and this is just the second chapter of this journey? We are merely beginning our journey together.

This is **1SELF**, reinvent yourself from any crisis.

To be faster than EVOLUTION,
To keep our RELEVANCY and FUN
Thanks to CONFIDENCE,
HUMILITY and INNOCENCE,

That's the journey ahead.
That's the promise of **1SELF**.

Dr. BAK NGUYEN

CHAPTER 3
THE TIME IS NOW

by Dr. BAK NGUYEN

Already, the time is now? At chapter 3?! I told you that we will be jazzing up this journey. Yes, the time is now. This is such a common phrase in the motivational world, to combat procrastination, the time is always now! But this time, more than ever, it is true. Please, allow me.

You are reading this as we, as a species, are at the crossroad of evolution, not just the awakening of one soul, but the future of our way of life, of existence, of communication. For the past three decades, technology and the means of communication have changed drastically the way we connect and communicate.

But until now, that was still on the surface, as old habits die hard, left alone our traditions and institutions. Well, it took a virus, a biological subform of Life to rewrite our code, in a matter of weeks, in a matter of months.

I am writing these lines as I am a witness and an actor of the digitalization of our world. Within the COVID war, all resistance got deflected to the war effort and the resistance to change vaporized, almost overnight. Everything is happening online and through a computer screen or a retina display, in high definition.

If our dependence on electricity and gas of the 20th century shaped the evolution, in the 21st century, it is our connectivity to the grid, our broadband, and bandwidth that are defining the power and influence ew now hold. Electricity is not enough, not anymore.

I realized that as my son was 2. He couldn't talk much but had, as a companion, my iPad, first-generation. Well, after all the food, the spit, and the biological liquids he spread all over it, the ownership of the iPad was clear. Well, at 2, he wasn't talking much but could tell me that the iPad ran out of battery. In fact, the battery was at 80%, it was the internet connection that went down.

It is then that I realized that it does not matter, a charged iPad without connection was useless to him. He was right, just bolder and without any filter. What is the world today, without connectivity? Without bandwidth?

Many would have argued that affirmation in 2012. By 2020, now entering 2021, who will survive a slower connection, left alone a limited bandwidth or an absence of network? We won't die, but frustration and depression will spike, overnight.

If we kept our heads down through the confinements, the masks, the curfews, the social distanciation, most of our hope and coping mechanisms turned to the web for a fix. And this is how the resistance to change vaporized within days.

All of those resisting change, are now pushing for it, easing the way and the transition. Now the resistance has been deflected to the front, to fight the invisible enemy, the virus.

What is this have to do with us rising? Really, do I have to answer that question? If at any time of my existence, I could write something universal, this is it. Whoever you are, where ever you are on the planet, this wave of viral change is changing you at your core!

> "The virus shut down all resistance.
> It also created a void for hope."
> Dr. Bak Nguyen

I am not debating the merits of the virus, simply citing the facts and consequences that it brought. And what hope are we talking about? Many, many hopes. Green peace activists will say that it allowed us to cut our addiction to fossil fuel.

The minimalists will cry victory over the break of our culture to over-consume… well, that's until our bandwidth made the founder of Amazon the richest man on earth, until the man behind the electric car took over. Is that real change, or just the new faces of our adapted, upgraded addictions?

I could go on for hours talking about how our society is adapting to face the COVID war. But I am more interested in here to see how you, how I, how we are experiencing the change.

Don't fool yourself by thinking that nothing has changed, everything has, now, faster than ever since there is no more resistance on the ground keeping change in check.

I used to be a progressive actor and agent of change. My title as I embraced the public scene the first time was as an disruptor. Can you imagine that now, I find myself behind the changes that our world is taking on as we are exchanging?!

That was at the beginning of the first confinement. Now within the second one, I have evolved, adapted, and upgraded. May my story give you the inspiration and confidence to find your way through this chaos.

10 months ago, I was back from Springbreak vacation and learned on the way home that a new virus has spread around the world. Before my departure, there were news about a virus in China, but that seemed so far away. It was business as usual.

I went back home, safe and healthy. But then, I got confront with news from the unreal, telling me to shut down all my professional activities overnight, for 2 weeks. We were in mid-March. I obeyed.

I had to reassure my team and my patients, not just mine, but the patients of my entire company. We all told ourselves that 2 weeks, that was no big deal.

Then, the schools closed down too. The shops shut down and the barriers started to appear. It was like living in a bad nightmare, one not too scary to wake up from, but one putting us unease the whole time. Even the sweat was not forming on your forehead, but your palms were wet. You know what I am talking about. We've all been there.

Well, after 2 weeks, we learned that the confinement will be extended to everyone for 2 more weeks. I remember the US president saying that by Easter, it will be over.

A couple of days later, it was extended to the beginning of May. As new cases and the death toll kept rising and piling up, I had the panic of my patients to ease, but also, I had my staff that was standing on the side with no means to understand how to cope.

I had connections, and before the lockdown, I promised them that I would be putting my connections at their services. So I did. I put aside my denial and waiting, and I picked up the phone.

Within hours, I was on the lines with officials and influence that could make or break the day. I helped as much as I could. They got my message, I was looking for assistance, for my people, for my peers, for my industry.

Then, I quickly realized how power and influence really work. I also noticed who has influence and who held empty titles. I did not hold any title, so to me, it was either influence or nothing. I learn about the new means of communication and went online, looking for connections and solutions.

Within days, I became a world anchor in my field and an influencer within the finance industry. From a dentist and a CEO looking to save his people and his company, I rose into a face that people recognize and a voice that people are listening to.

Sure, I was on that rise before COVID, but that was local, walking up the streets of downtown and having people greeting me. Now, it was International. I was International.

Slowly, the people I interviewed and connected with became the organization we now know as **THE ALPHAS**. My interviews became shows and international summits. I had people joining in who invented technologies that changed my life and yours.

Amongst the first people I met was Dr. Paul Ouellette, an orthodontist with 50 years of experience. He and I became friends very quickly. He introduced his friends, Dr. Robert Boyd, the man who lead the advent of clear and digitilized orthodontics. Part of my success revolves around his work!

I interviewed my mentor and friend, Christian Trudeau, the man who digitalized the Montreal Stock Exchange, the man who was talking about e-commerce and payment solutions when we were still talking about TCP-IP, in the early 90s. He created billions in value for Bell Canada as the former CEO and founder of BCE Emergis.

I interviewed André Châtelain, another friend and mentor who was the former number 2 of one of our big financial institutions in Quebec, managing hundreds of billions. André is the former first vice-president of the Mouvement Desjardins.

Amongst celebrities, I had the chance to interview a friend and influencer, Dr. Anil Gupta, the personal happiness coach of Mike Tyson, a friend of Sir Richard Branson, and of Anthony Robbins. Anil joined me to share his recipe for immediate happiness. He is on the quest to touch one billion souls!

I had the pleasure to receive on-air, Ron Klein, an American inventor who invented the magnetic stripe of the credit card. He also invented MLS, the multi-listing system which is now the core of the real estate brokerage industry. Mr. Klein also digitalized Wall Street's Bond market.

I also had the pleasure to welcome Dr. Sylvain Guimond on the show. Dr. Guimond has treated most of the biggest names in the Sports Industry: Mario Lemieux, Tiger Woods, Governor Schwarzenegger and so many more.

Lately, I welcomed my old friend and mentor, Dr. Jean De Serres, the former head of the equivalent of the Red-Cross in Quebec, Hema Quebec on-air, as an Alpha.

I interviewed hundreds of people. Some I knew, some I just met. These gentlemen I cited up there were the most prominent names, but I had presidents of company, politicians, and heads of industries joining me. They all accepted my invitation to come and to share in order for all of us to cope and to heal.

After healing, rebuilding and reinventing were next on the table. We covered subjects as diverse as the digitalization of dentistry, shifting the political paradigm on air, to the emergence of Black Lives Matter, looking for peace. I was playing my part, to empower great minds to share, and to empower each of us to find our better self, to find hope and salvation.

Well, I was also on a stream of world records, writing books before the COVID war. Well, even if I kept writing, I lost my focus and could not maintain my speed. So instead of writing 2 books a month, I started to write and to direct international collaborations with thinkers, movers, and shakers around the world. We wrote and published within record time, usually within weeks.

By the end of June, I realized, on-air, that I would have to write a book every 8 days for the next 8 weeks straight to score my next world record of writing 72 books within 36 months. Well, I said that on-air and I started writing. Please note that by June, I was also resuming my business, trying to keep my company from financial ruin.

Well, thousands of people watched that interview as I was saying that I will have to write a book every 8 days for 8 weeks. Well, they followed my tracks as I was writing a chapter after the next. I ended up writing a book every 8 days on average for 8 weeks straight and I scored my 72nd book 10 days before the dateline!

Actually, it was even better than that. I lied! I did not write a book every 8 days for 8 weeks straight finishing with 10 days in advance, I published a book every 8 days for 8 weeks straight! From the end of July to the end of August that year, Amazon published 6 of my books, the latest!

A few weeks after, Barnes and Noble welcomed me into their library. I was now a published author, one self-rising through the ranks of the big world of publishing. Actually, now that I joined Barnes and Noble, the biggest books outlet in the United-States of America with 1.3 billion in annual sales, I elevated myself into a publishing company too!

Those were huge victories and honors. I am still too busy to write my next book to stop and to submit my work to the Guinness world record, but I've done it, and people are now following my track daily, as I announce my chapters and books, one after the next.

By Fall that year, I was honored and recognized as one of the world TOP100 doctors of 2021. That came in for my efforts and achievements to inspire my profession.

For someone who never wanted to be a doctor in the first place, that was surely a huge recognition. Yes, I became a doctor to honor my parents. Today, I am bearing the title to honor them, but also to remind myself that I always have to put your interests before mine. This is what I learn, becoming a doctor for the last 20 years.

Well, this is sure a great story to tell, a true story. (you can research the web to confirm the facts). That being said, the point I wanted to make here is that I went online and announce myself boldly and with confidence.

I did so to find answers for all of us, not only for myself. I did so by empowering the great overachievers in front of me. They all loved me for that. And they shared their secrets and philosophy, openly, freely, so all of us could find inspiration and hope.

Then, I talked openly about my crazy challenges and I walked my talk, in the public eye. Even the naysayers and non-believers followed my journey. And I got the recognitions coming with the achievements.

Looking back, I am so far away from where I started, 4 years ago, as I first embraced a public life and the stage. I am still the same person, but this time, the resistance is gone. I announced and I delivered.

Well, I did that all of my life, but now it was spotted by the leaders, the industries, and the crowd. My recipe was very simplistic: talk boldly, clearly, and walk your talk!

In other words, I announced who I want to be and became that person, walking my talk in the eye of the public. Today, I am a world anchor and a personality, and this is not even my wording, but the wording of those interviewing me.

So this is the hope that I am bringing to you. Today, more than ever, at the crossroad of the evolution of our society, you can be who you want to be. You can rise and become the person you feel inside.

Announce yourself and walk your talk. Shortly, you will grow into that person who, today, you are convincing yourself not to forget. If I have done it, so can you.

And before we jump to another subject, do you want to know a secret? Back in June, I had no idea if I could write a book every 8 days for 8 weeks straight. In the back of my mind, even if I fail, I would have scored a new world record, an odd one like 67 books written over the course of 3 years, or 71. Every book I now write is a new world record, but I like the rounded numbers.

That being said, I took my own words very seriously and I ran as if my life depended on it. I ended up scoring even much more than I originally projected as an impossible goal.

Well, you know what? I did it with ease and without putting the rest of my life on hold. At the same time, I was present as never before as a dentist on the ground, and multiplying my intervention in world summits.

I even managed to successfully stir my enterprise to good safe shores, navigating the financial tsunami of COVID. I did that with the help of my partner, Tranie Vo, and with the support of my team. I got help, but I was there to support and to rally each of them, on the ground.

Well, while we are on the confidences, I have to tell you that within the talks behind the scenes of **THE ALPHAS**, I am looking at the opportunity to create 2 new companies, an international investment fund and the question of a movie studio and an animation studio are floating in the air.

Does that make any sense to any of you? I can tell you that it does not make sense to me either. But this is from the perspective of someone looking up at the events, afterward.

Being at the center of the storm, I can tell you each of the steps and the logic behind each choice and action. That makes much sense, what does not is the perspective looking up at the trail and its consequences.

So here is the inspiration of the day: stop fearing the storm ahead. Stop being worried about things out of your control. Once you get rid of those anxiety and doubts clouding your horizon, the path is clear, right in front of you.

If you need a push, well, leverage the social network and announce your move before doing them. Doing so, you are putting yourself back to the wall, with no choice but to actually walk your talk.

Talk boldly and you will have to walk fast, to learn on the way, and to grow into that person you said you were. Do that under the eye of the public, and you have successfully fight procrastination and excuses.

Wait, there is more! The cherry on top is that you won't even have to spend on marketing, they were following you live, unfiltered. Now they are believers, and you? You are walking your legend! The time is now!

This is **1SELF,** reinvent yourself from any crisis.

To be faster than EVOLUTION,
To keep our RELEVANCY and FUN
Thanks to CONFIDENCE,
HUMILITY and INNOCENCE,

That's the journey ahead.
That's the promise of **1SELF**.

Dr. BAK NGUYEN

CHAPTER 4
THE FORGE

by Dr. BAK NGUYEN

You have no idea how unsettling writing this book is to me. I told you that we will be jazzing up this one. Well, since the beginning of the writing, I wrote without a plan in mind. Actually, the book I had in mind was covered within the last 3 chapters.

I wasn't cheap, I gave you all that I had. But now, I risk the danger of facing the white page syndrome every morning, wondering what to write and what to share with you.

> "I told you that I am walking my talk!"
> Dr. Bak Nguyen

The reason I jazzed up my proven writing process is because I like to be genuine with you. To reinvent oneself is about feeling, not about thinking. So even if I've walked that path before, what I would be writing would be my reflections and souvenirs moving through, not my actual feelings.

So, as I am inviting you to jump off the cliff of safety and of the known, I am leading the charge, jumping ahead too.

> "It is never too late to reinvent ourselves,
> it never gets old either."
> Dr. Bak Nguyen

That's the coolest part of the journey. You can try and taste and change your mind. Then, you can jump again, only now, you have more insurance and have a better idea of what to expect. Not to have expectations since that might limit and spoil your journey. But you have a vague idea of how you will be reacting to the new!

And that's enough to me, to know how I will embrace the new, not knowing what new it would be nor how I will face it, only that I am ready to face it, to learn and to adapt, once more. It is by jumping again and again, that I came to throw away most of my pride and medals, they aren't helping in the journey ahead.

It is very true what they say: The more you learn, the less you know. My former coach and mentor told me once that I should be aiming at **BEING**, not at **HAVING**. Since I am throwing away the medals each time that I am jumping, I know that all that I can take with me, every single time, is what I am, what I learn and my confidence facing the new.

And this will prove to be of great use to any of us. Forget being strong, forget being smart, those are only true within a rigid reference frame. If you want to thrive in the new, you must embrace flexibility and swiftness.

> "Success will depend on how much can one adapt and how fast one can do so."
> Christian Trudeau

This is what, at the beginning of the first confinement a man who created billions in value shared with me and the world: how fast can you adapt? To put things in context, it was about facing the COVID crisis and how each of us should react to find footing.

That being said, isn't that the key wisdom of anyone reinventing him or herself? To adapt swiftly. Even if you do not have all the parameters of the equation, adapt with what you have and learn and to reassess on the way.

And this is me talking. Since it wasn't too much information to compile at first, it is easy to assimilate those quickly, if you do not invite doubt to the table. Then, look for a quick win, as small as it may be. Look for a quick win and test your theory and information gathering.

Most of the time, the information was accurate, you only need to rearrange its order and to link the dots differently. The flexibility is your ability to rearrange the dots and how you link them, no one can change reality, but everyone can have his or her own perception of reality. And this is what it is, to be flexible enough to alter your perception of reality.

Going for a win, as quickly as possible, will also have another great effect. It will build up your confidence and reinforce positively your flexibility and swiftness. Strong and smart do not always win, speed and adaptation will, every single time.

Those aren't knowledge that I've polished before presenting to you, there are still hot on the plate I am serving you, because those are right out of the forge, once again. You see, I am scoring world record after world record because I have fun doing so.

I got good writing, but who would want to write the same thing over and over again. That boredom would bury me alive! And yet, this is how we become good at something, by doing it again and again.

Well, I found a way to leverage both of these opposites and to yield both their powers at the same time. I jump the cliff, again and again, becoming better at each jump.

Yes, each jump is unique, but you get to find the same ingredient eventually. So I jazzed it up by melting my tools, even my best ones before each jump.

I am forging new tools from the raw material of the last ones. I am forging my tool as I am mid-air between the cliff and the ground. That's much pressure, but that's also where my mind will operate without pride or blindspot, to forge the tools I will need now to surf this new jump.

By tools, I meant mindsets. Doing so, I am forcing myself to evolve at the pace of change itself, even if I have forced the hand of Fate to impose change, once more.

Now the only thing that I keep is the insurance that I will be learning something new, even forging the same tool once more. Now, it is better, lighter and also, different, somehow.

> "Your mindsets are the results of your experiences. They have an expiration date and a status of limitation, within the boundaries of that journey. There are so many other journeys ahead."
> Dr. Bak Nguyen

So back at the writing of this journey without a plan. Well, by not holding back and by sharing with you everything that I planned within the first 3 chapters, I allowed myself the space of 5 new chapters to discover new horizons and wisdom and fun.

Because this is what is keeping the fun in the equation, the surprises and the unknown are what's keeping the excitement. That, and the first small win.

Within the first 3 chapters of this journey, you heard me sharing my journey, well, I was inspecting each piece of my armor and mindset before throwing them in the fire of the forge. I was that genuine with you because I was saying farewell to my tools and mindsets. At least, that version of them.

I threw in the fire the tools I knew about this journey. I kept my heart open and made myself available to listen, once more. I listen to the wind, to the birds, to the clouds and the sun. I made myself available without prejudice since all of them are now melting in the forge.

And the result coming out is always something unexpected. Just like this chapter, it is as hot as hell, hot, and smoking. This new version of my mindset, reinventing myself just got a little better from my previous version, which I still stand by.

No, I am not looking for perfection, I am looking for new and for fun. And to be fun, I must keep my heart and mind open. Maybe that's why I got along so well with my kid because I still have that elasticity and flexibility natural to kids.

Well, rest assured, you too can gain back that flexibility and elasticity of your mind by throwing your tools and mindsets in the forge. Do that often and you will be stronger than ever, smarter than never before because now, you are flexible.

I know, it does not sound very reassuring, walking the unknown without any known tool. The first time, keep your tools and mindsets intact. Walking the way, you will sort them out, one by one.

Remember, to look at the storm from the outside and looking up at it, just gave you one perspective of the storm, maybe the worst perspective.

From closer, the storm, any storm, is not as dark, nor as dense. And once inside, once your senses start to adapt to the new conditions, it was just another walk to finish. Different, but still a walk.

And swiftly? Well, that was doing yourself the biggest of favors, not paralyzing yourself standing in front of the storm and making false ideas about what you will find inside.

You don't know what you don't know. And the more time you will be preparing, guessing the unknown, the harder it will be for you to throw those in the forge as you need the resources once on your path.

What I am not melting, is my heart. That I know the beating and rhythm. That is keeping me secured to be flexible and open, and still confident of the outcome. What I am melting is what was laying in my head.

And you know what, after a few jumps, most of my doubt and pride, once melt, never resurface. I am not saying that I am *doubtfree* nor *pridefree*, but the fire purged most of the doubt and pride I had.

Something to notice, as I am writing this chapter, my dictionary is telling me that **doubtfree** and **pridefree** are not words from the English known dictionary. Do you have any idea of what I am about to say next? Well, you just have a concrete example of what is it to melt down your mindset in order to forge new ones.

And I am not sure what the next chapter will be about. I just know that it will have to be better than this one, which, by far, was better and more genuine than the first three… I can't wait to discover it with you.

This is **1SELF,** reinvent yourself from any crisis.

To be faster than EVOLUTION,
To keep our RELEVANCY and FUN
Thanks to CONFIDENCE,
HUMILITY and INNOCENCE,

That's the journey ahead.
That's the promise of **1SELF**.

Dr. BAK NGUYEN

CHAPTER 5
SMALL WINS ARE HUGE

by Dr. BAK NGUYEN

Rising up and reinventing ourselves is a lonely path. Be warned. Unless you have the support of a coach who initiated the awakening, you are doing that on your own, and everyone you know will be discouraging you to rise up.

All of them will be telling you to resume your post in life. And those are the people closest to you, who cared enough to say something. Well, no one likes change, once they have sorted you and labeled you in their awareness, it is very unsettling for them to have to reassess you. Don't blame them, you are doing the same to any of them.

That being said, you have to know that the path to reinvent yourself is a very lonely one. When I told you that the demons on the way wear familiar faces, this is part of what I meant… until jealousy kicks in later on, but that is another story, one for another chapter.

In classic literature and human history, it is said that to have the courage to face an enemy is great. Greater is to have the strength to stand up to our friends. And this is your journey, reinventing yourself, rising: to face your family and friends.

That fight will be dragging you the whole time you will be cocooning and trying to define yourself. My only advice here, is to focus on you and on your transformation. In most situations, the change we are undergoing often originated from our love for someone else, for them.

Focus on that, on the **WHY** you are cocooning and reforging your values and goals. Otherwise, you will let **Doubt** drown you with your own thoughts. Once you have undergone the process to reinvent yourself, stop looking for permission and approval, you are looking for real answers, not opinions.

Keep this close to your heart.

Trust me, I've spent years trying to do this without breaking any eggs. It is a field of eggshells, all important to you and there are laying in all the directions. There is no way to do this with harmony and consensus. Well, this is what I got wrong the first time.

> "The consensus you need is one with yourself."
> Dr. Bak Nguyen

You need to align your will and your desire so you can emerge whole, one, and powerful. This is what you are doing, cocooning, and melting your values, identity, and goals. Of course, those who knew will think that you've lost your mind, you are melting away everything that they shared with you. Of course, they will try to stop you.

But this was about you, your life, your decision, your future. And this is what you need to understand first, so you can smile at them and close that door until your transformation is completed.

It will take much courage and strength to close that door to the smiles, the tears, and the love. You are not doing it out of selfishness nor cruelty, you are doing it so you can find your whole, your footing, and connection with Nature, with yourself. Ever wanted a **me-time**? Well, this is your ultimate **me-time**!

That being said, you just cut yourself from any exterior support and help possible. Now, you are left alone facing yourself, your doubts, and your own desires. I can tell you that it is very, very unsettling and disorientating. So how can you find footing?

Long ago, I learned that thinking will never solve a mystery. If anything, the more one thinks, the more questions will arise. And the smarter the thinker, the more abundant the questions! The only way to find answers and to understand them fully is to walk the path.

That's what you will have to do, to walk that path even if you do not know where it is leading nor if it is the right path for you. On that, allow me to help you.

> "The path is the one in front of you.
> It is for you to set it right."
> Dr. Bak Nguyen

Your other option is to refuse that path and to stand your ground, hoping that the ground will not be shifting beneath your feet. And since earthquakes are not happening daily, you think that you are safe.

Well, wrong again! Scientists will tell you that the planet is rotating around the sun and pivoting on itself. Even the surface of the planet is shifting, almost surfing over the planet's magma. So no, nothing ever standstill.

And this is the first acceptation that you will need to make peace with, nothing ever stands still, you are just too little to comprehend its movement. This is not bad at all for a first day cocooning, understanding that nothing ever standstill and that we are little.

And understanding those will free you from the opinions and peer pressure of those you are attached to. You are cocooning to grow from that littleness, to comprehend a little better the dynamics of the Universe and of Life. You can't do that standing still! In other words, you cannot grow, staying the same!

And peace will start to settle in your heart. Listen to your heartbeat, even if you were insecure facing the unknown, it is beating calmly and strongly. You are now listening to yourself. That was your first win of the journey, to hear yourself.

> "Aim for your next win, as small as it might be.
> Aim for that win as quickly as possible."
> Dr. Bak Nguyen

I would love to tell you that you have all the time in the world to peacefully travel your transformation, but that will be a lie, at least from what I know. Since we are all taking a break from our present existence to steal time for ourselves, time is not on our side.

How many times can you close that door to those smiling back and you? How many times can you close that door to these tears of love? For your own sake, you will need to find answers to justify your decision and behavior, trying to find yourself.

Soon enough, your own personal doubts will be threatening the whole process, unless you have moved swiftly enough to be different, to understand enough to change, even if it was by a tiny bit.

Well, that change you are looking for is that small win, one that will justify your journey, one that will boost your confidence, and one that will reinforce your will to keep pushing forward.

> "In the solitude of your cocoon, your only reference points now are your next wins."
> Dr. Bak Nguyen

And to win what? Well, to test your new mindsets, facing an event with either the absence of your own mindset or the application of the new one. Test it and see how you are reacting. By reacting, I meant how you are feeling. If the feeling is right, you are on the right path and that's your win.

If not, well, try something else. It was simply an exercise! That word, **exercise**, will help you tremendously to travel your journey since it will obliterate the expectation of perfection. An exercise is meant to be learned from and to adapt and to be better. Well, well, well, isn't that the recipe for success?

And that win will change you from the inside out. You'll be surprised how a small win can erase the biggest of doubts. You'll be surprised how a small win can harmonize the storm of change into a peaceful flow.

Feel it to understand, feel it to find peace and harmony.

And do that quickly since Time wasn't on your side, until the first win. Now, win after win, even Time will be kind since everyone loves to be on the winning side. Well, never before, doubt was on the winning side.

Only with a win, will you open the door and greet those you left behind, for a moment. You are different. And they will be too. The dynamic has changed, but now, you have something to hold on to, your feeling of harmony inside.

Now you can continue your transformation outside of your cocoon. This is called rising!

This is **1SELF**, reinvent yourself from any crisis.

To be faster than EVOLUTION,
To keep our RELEVANCY and FUN
Thanks to CONFIDENCE,
HUMILITY and INNOCENCE,

That's the journey ahead.
That's the promise of **1SELF**.

Dr. BAK NGUYEN

CHAPTER 6
THE CATERPILLAR EFFECT

by Dr. BAK NGUYEN

It would be so nice to have the time, in our evolution and life, to come to a stop, to cocoon, and to rise from a caterpillar into a butterfly and fly away. Even if the comparison stands and makes much sense, we do not have that luxury to cocoon up for long and to emerge with wings.

Just like a caterpillar, once inside of the cocoon, everything is melting and morphing, changing physically into something else, something new, something different. Once in cocoon mode, it is when we are the most vulnerable, having no physical shape.

Well, what is the cocoon in real life? Your desire to find yourself and your will to see it through. In other words, your **WHY**, and your **Confidence**. It is a pretty thin layer of protection will you say.

Confidence is a very abstract concept. Too thick and it is blind pride and arrogance. Too thin and it is useless. How do you solve such an equation? By putting someone else at the center of your journey.

You are the one walking, but you did it for someone else. By doing so, you are personifying your WHY and giving it a face and a name. That will help tremendously.

Having someone else at the heart of your rise isn't deflecting, it is in fact very empowering. We've spent our entire life hearing not to be selfish. But how can one grow and focus on him or herself if thinking about him or herself was forbidden and wrong to start with? Do the same, while thinking for someone else.

More than defeating the scams of peer pressures and of cultural and folkloric beliefs, you will be insuring that you are building Confidence and desire, while keeping the doors open because you grew from compassion.

"The only way to emerge from the cocoon with wings was by focussing on oneself. The only way to grow these wings was to be greater than one."
Dr. Bak Nguyen

And how are you doing that, to be greater than one? By loving someone else and to be better for that person. If you are coming back to the Pyramid of Maslow, it might be simpler to understand the concept.

Before your awakening, you were in the mid-level, at the level of love and belonging. Belonging, it was also why it was so hard to take off from that level. Belonging means to settle, to average, and to be accepted and to accept.

Well, everything you did on your path to evolution led in a straight line to that path, so why now is there a glass ceiling? Because of **Belonging**.

But Abraham Maslow described something else at that layer too, love. So if you concentrate on your love for someone, and that love outgrows the belonging values, you just create a pathway for your awakening.

You will have to cocoon somewhere between the layers of **ESTEEM** and **BELONGING**, but you will have risen above the glass ceiling holding you down for so long.

To me, fatherhood was that path. The day my son was born, that day, I started my awakening, out of pure love for him. I did not want to forge him the way that I've been forged. I did not want to pressure him and to risk breaking him. I, myself, still am carrying the scars on my back. I wanted to love and to enjoy the journey with him.

So I decided not to forge him. I decided to forge myself into the man I would love him to become. That way, the pressure was on me and not on him. I would change and hope that he will copy what he sees.

Ten years down that path, I never broke his spirit in the name of education, I never clip his wings to ease control, I never even told him what to be. I showed him freewill and consequences. That worked like a charm.

I inspire him, I connect with him. At 5, he inspired me back to create **eHappyPedia**, the encyclopedia of happiness, a project that is now on the launchpad to become my next breakthrough. At 7, he wanted to write books with me, and those are his own words. At 8, he held several world records, co-authoring 22 books with me.

Today, we are the best of buddies. For those of you intrigued by this fairy tale, the whole story, the true story is told in the **BOOK OF LEGENDS** volume one and two. Many times before, I was looking to break free, but never, I could overcome the glass ceiling. Doing it in the name of love, the transition was flawless, without resistance.

I was a dentist who became a doctor to honor his immigrant parents, one with a failed dream of becoming a Hollywood movie producer.

By myself, I was stuck between **rebelling** or **belonging**. I was in a loop for nearly a decade. I had love, but that love also came with much belonging. The birth of William took belonging and elevated it into a **responsibility status**. And to embody that responsibility, I changed, I rose.

> "The love for my son melted the glass ceiling."
> Dr. Bak Nguyen

I did not cocoon for long. I did that the early mornings, looking at sunrise while feeding him. I compensated for my lack of sleep with the warmth of both the sunlight on my face and the body heat of his tiny body sleeping, once his belly was full. I melted my beliefs and values and became the man I was wishing him to become.

Well, I rose from a dentist to a CEO, one with influence and the favor of the financial world. I then rose from CEO to world record author. Today, I don't know what I am, just a man having fun sharing, a man free and happy.

I cocooned within these early mornings. I rose. Always keeping the idea of becoming the man I hope my son will grow into. Well, I never took a time off. On the contrary, I built companies and clinics. With the help of my partner, best friend, and wife, we materialize our dreams and visions into structures and products.

In theory, I was doubling down on my commitment as a doctor, but somehow, it did not felt like signing a new contract, it felt more like it was always meant to be.

This is how, as I signed a contract with myself to be the best dentist for 10 years and to reevaluate my options after, I overran that expiration date by 8 years without any regrets. I did so, focussed, committed, and free. I did so while emerging as a visionary businessman and a philosopher writing at a world record pace.

If you would have told me that I would become an author 10 years ago, I would be the first to laugh. I guess, I owe my luck to fate and to have stayed open to listen. And that's is the transformation and the rise.

In real life situation, we do not take a time off to reinvent ourselves, we do it on the fly while keeping the other pieces of our lives balanced. We need to find our WHY and to start changing, even with a single degree, our angle and take about Life. And then, we keep marching each day, day after day.

My WHY was the love for my son. My will was my discipline and dedication to change and to walk that change. Every day, as I hold William, I was reminded of my WHY. Looking at him growing, I was also reminded of how fast he was growing. I needed to match that pace, or even better, to be faster.

To advance was not a concern anymore. The speed was not a concern either. It was all about the pace of my acceleration. And it is how I am known today on the world stage, as a force of nature, a tornado, and a momentum. Well, to me, I was just walking my next journey and the one after.

> "Rising isn't a moment, but an era."
> Dr. Bak Nguyen

At the end of the last chapter, I told you that you are now rising. Well, you are, but it is for you to keep fuelling your momentum and your WHY. We do not have the luxury of the caterpillar effect to cocoon for a while and to become perfect before we can spread our wings.

We awake and we walk, with patches and imperfections. The only thing we have is the will to be better, it is the awareness of our own imperfections. Well, even that is a great plan! I told you to look for your first win. Look at the small imperfection you see in the mirror and change that one. Then, move on to the next one.

Soon enough, you will not have just polish yourself, but at the falling of each imperfection, you are changing from the inside out.

You see, each imperfection requires its own attention and set of rules. Every time you drop one imperfection, you are also dropping the system coming with it. And much sooner than you think, you are freeing much-needed resources to keep pushing forward.

> "The dumping of your imperfections will free much energy and resource to feed your journey."
> Dr. Bak Nguyen

Not just your imperfections, but the lies and the expectations too! Both those can only be addressed once you have built up enough confidence and freed enough resources to tackle. A small win at a time, and keep pushing. That's your path to rise.

So, you do not have to be the brightest nor the strongest, you just need to find your WHY and to walk that path every day with an open heart and mind to learn on the way. To **learn** and to **readjust** on the way are the keywords for those looking for a clear recipe.

And what new did this chapter brought to the table? Well, to forget about the perfect timing, to forget about finding enough time to start, and, ultimately, to forget about finding the perfect recipe before awakening. It is a process and everything is happening on the way, walking, not thinking.

You are rising up stepping on your successes and mistakes. You keep rising because your desire to be better and genuine outweighed your need to belong and to conform. That was rising up.

To awake, that was your first victory. To find your WHY, the second one. Now, how about a win a day to start the pace of your journey? The fun is in the walk. Look at this on the bright side, you won't have to be a caterpillar for much longer and the cocoon phase is already over. That was when you were most vulnerable.

Now, you are stretching your wings and exercising them every day to strengthen their reach and range, a win at a time.

This is **1SELF,** reinvent yourself from any crisis.

To be faster than EVOLUTION,
To keep our RELEVANCY and FUN
Thanks to CONFIDENCE,
HUMILITY and INNOCENCE,

That's the journey ahead.
That's the promise of **1SELF**.

Dr. BAK NGUYEN

CHAPTER 7
OVERACHIEVING

by Dr. BAK NGUYEN

What a ride. As you are rising, I am sharing the thrill with you. I envy you, that feeling of excitement of discovering your powers for the first time. I am still discovering new powers almost daily, but the first time, that's always very special.

That being said, now that you have awoken, that you are growing while rising, how about some pointers to ease your transition?

BE OPEN

Keep both your mind and heart open to grow, that's the fastest way. By keeping your heart open, you are growing but not solely for yourself. Putting love and compassion at the center of your journey, you are strengthening your **WHY** and you are gaining power since more people attracted by the same cause might join you as allies for a while.

> "Rising is a lonely path unless you are rising with and from compassion."
> Dr. Bak Nguyen

Find others to serve, to service. The more people you are helping, the stronger you will grow. The more people you are helping at the same time, the faster your growth.

While they might benefit from your work, you are the only recipient of the experience since you will be the one growing with all you will have to do to learn and master to service them. From a service relationship, the one growing is rarely the one of the receiving end, but the giving.

> "Sharing is the way to grow."
> Dr. Bak Nguyen

I said that since my first book. Because I shared, I finished a book. Because I shared, I kept writing. Today, I am a world record author, thanks to the power of sharing. This is the shortest way for me to prove my point to you.

The more people you are helping, the bigger will be your influence. And trust me, influence is power without resistance! While rising, the strongest force you will find against you is the resistance to change, both from the people holding you back and your roots, but also your doubt and indecision, pinning you down.

That lockdown is the most dangerous situation for someone rising. It can break you, and your spirit, if you are standing too long between the pressure and the tension. Don't try to balance this one. And standing still, well, that could kill you.

That was exactly what we all fear, to be strip naked and vulnerable, and to be torn apart under the public eye. The best way for you to escape from that fatal fate was to open your mind.

Not everyone has a cause at the beginning of their rise. That's okay, that's normal. Try embracing the first one coming, even if you do not believe in it. You know that rising and freshly out of the cocoon, you are vulnerable and time is not on your side, so forget about the due diligence, that's a luxury that might kill you.

My advice is to take the opportunity as an exercise. Just make sure that you are helping and not causing any harm. And see how you can help. Most of the time, they will need something that you cannot provide. Well, ask yourself, how can you try?

Remember, this is an exercise for you, nothing more and nothing less. Give it your best shot and see how it feels. Give it a day or two, and see what you've learnt. You'll be surprised by how much more you were capable of.

Keeping an open mind and open heart was the easiest and fastest way for you to not standstill on the hot plate of your rise. And you know what? Well, helping people also have the benefit of cleansing your emotions.

When you are looking to correct your own imperfection, you are doing that bathing in your own emotions, everything is important and nothing can be stripped away unless it can. Well, when you applied yourself to helping others, that emotional component is not present, at least not from your end. It becomes much easier to learn and to master new skills and ideas.

Give it a try to feel its power. Rise with an open heart and an open mind.

> "Influence is power without resistance."
> Dr. Bak Nguyen

TIME FRAME

I did that, saying YES to virtually every proposal I got for 18 months, resetting my mind and standards. This is how I got rid of my habit of judging and labeling people. People are what they are, it doesn't mean that I have to take that into me.

I helped when I could. Even if I could not, I was forced to say YES, so I tried first, giving it my best shot. My protection was that I usually give a very short time frame for each exercise: 2 weeks. I give my best for 2 weeks and then, I know that I will have to move on to the next exercise.

Well, that 2 weeks window became the main ingredient of my **power of momentum**. I have 2 weeks to understand, to find leverage, and to deliver results. I won't succeed every time and I made my peace with that. That being said, I am still convinced that I will have a chance to score a win within the next 2 weeks.

Call it the beginner's luck, call it intelligence, I don't care. But the more diverse subjects I got involved in, the more I grew, and much much faster than I could ever have anticipated. I went from being a dentist to help bridge the stemcell's national policy. I did that in a record time (2 months) and jealousy got the best of the deal, but that is a story for another day.

I accepted the proposal to become a speaker, inspiring entrepreneurs. Well, this is how I became accidentally a writer. If this is an area where I keep my 2 weeks time frame, it is writing books. I have a short attention span, so 2 weeks for a book and then, I move on to another subject, the more different and diverse, the better!

I became an overachiever just because I could not say no to anything. I became a force of nature because I was determined to score a win. I grew because every time, I learn and master new skills and developed new perspectives without resistance.

SYNERGY

"Build from the differences."
Dr. Jean De Serres

Even with people joining your vibe and wanting to be part of your journey rising, it still remains a lonely path. Mostly, people are coming in to have their piece of cake, not to pitch in. Give it to them, the growth happened on the giving end, remember?

But some times, not every time, but some times, you will meet some people like you, looking to help and to rise. Not all of them will be sharing your views nor your time frame, but they will gladly accept your help and contribution.

Don't come in wanting to reinvent the wheel. The goal was to move fast and without resistance. But don't come in and listen to the story of their lives, their regrets and aspirations either. You only have 2 weeks, time is of the essence.

Politely, narrow down the conversation to a problem deserving a specific population. The more specific, the better. You have just established a goal.

If that goal cannot be achieved within 2 weeks, well, keep narrowing down the question until you might have a way to solve it within days, not weeks. You'll be surprised how even a small win, within 2 weeks, can change the vibe of an entire cause!

> "In a hurry, be the key and
> let the system to others."
> Dr. Bak Nguyen

And this, I've done more than once, to be the key, the catalyst instead of the entirety of the system. Thanks to that, I do not have to be perfect, to look for perfection nor to criticize anyone.

I just solve my narrow piece of the puzzle and give them a boost in moral and inspiration. My involvement was punctual, everyone knows that from the beginning.

And since I am not there to stay, it becomes very natural to find relays and people to pass the baton. Most of the time, you will try to find someone like you, but within 2 weeks, that's impossible, you do not have that time nor luxury. So you have to open up with the people present.

One of the people I met within that 2 weeks mind frame, on the field, is Dr. Jean De Serres. We were, and still are, 2 very, very different people. What is uniting us was the will to score a win. Well, we gave it our best and we learned to respect one another on the field.

To build from the differences with respect, this is the wisdom that Dr. De Serres will be writing in our book together, many years after the facts. You can read it in **THE RISE OF THE UNICORN** that we co-wrote together.

What started as diverse and non reconciliable, we build from it. After all, life is created when two opposites are in contact.

And the only way to make it work is to open up and to listen. Then, you have established the dots of the equation.

Now, be open trying to link and to unlink and to relink them, creatively. You'll be having much fun doing so if you were not looking to be right, but to be useful. And that's respect. Otherwise, the resistance of pride will crush everything.

And it is very true. The more diverse the problems and the people, the more interesting the equation and the creative solutions. I learn beyond any expectation embracing the exercises of diversity with a 2 weeks mind-frame.

Today, I approach almost all projects and propositions with the same mindset. I wish that the 2 weeks mind-frame could be applied everywhere, but now, everyone knows my expectations, and we a negotiating. That's a huge win, if you ask me!

If you wanted the secret to **OVERACHIEVING**, I just gave you one! Take everything as an exercise. Give it 2 weeks and your best. Listen to the difference and build with respect. You do not have to solve the whole system, start with the key, and let others take over.

And from awakening, you rose. From rosing, now you are surfing changes, changing the world and overachieving with much fun.

This is **1SELF**, reinvent yourself from any crisis.

To be faster than EVOLUTION,
To keep our RELEVANCY and FUN
Thanks to CONFIDENCE,
HUMILITY and INNOCENCE,

That's the journey ahead.
That's the promise of **1SELF**.

Dr. BAK NGUYEN

CHAPTER 8
JEALOUSY

by Dr. BAK NGUYEN

How can I delay that subject further? In the previous chapters, we talked about jealousy and its ugly face. By now, I think that we are ready to face jealousy and its familiar faces.

I will be forward with you, I hate this part of the journey. Talking about others is just not my forte. Sure, without attachment, jealousy will not affect you, but the truth is that before we can cut our anchors, we must face them first.

To cut your attachment and anchors, to free them from you and you from them, you must understand why. The noble reason is to allow yourself to rise. But that will not suffice to convince you since loyalty, love, and attachments are the cores of our beliefs.

I guessed we became that way with the advent of agriculture and sedentarism. We became settlers, looking to own more than to be… free. From that, we perverted our wording and philosophy, measuring the world and ourselves from what we hold, from what we control.

You wanted to know why we are so little? How much can you see? How much can you hold? How much can you have? Those are the boundaries of the settler's philosophy.

> "And we exchange freedom for security."
> Dr. Bak Nguyen

This is a recurring theme in our modern society. But the origin goes back much earlier and much deeper. It came from settling. Please, don't get me wrong, there is nothing wrong about settling and looking for security, those were the base of our evolution (see the pyramid of Maslow).

That is also why in the middle of the pyramid, we all hit the glass ceiling. And then, we spent years walking around, not understanding why we ceased to evolve. Well, now we know that the only way through the glass ceiling was through the cocoon, as we are melting away what brought us so far and to forge new values, new tools for the journey ahead.

Once done, the first thing that we would want to do is to liberate all those we love who stayed behind. Wrong! If from your perspective, you were trying to liberate and help them; to them, you are a fool menacing their roots and all they cherish their entire life. Love will become hate. Friends will become enemies. And you will have become a traitor.

From their perspective, they are perfectly right. How about you? Well, even if you understand these values, you melted them away in the cocoon and survived the process. Why would you keep around values not vital to your path, happiness, or freedom? I'll let you answer that question.

So eventually, you will understood that going back and forcing your enlightenment is not a good idea. You cannot help someone before he or she is ready and has asked for your help. All you can do is to leave hints and your old tools on the way, so they will find them and figure out for themselves what to make of them.

I am saying your old tools because most you will melt, but some will have so much history that you will not throw them in the fire. Those, you will be polishing, cleaning, and leaving as treasures for others to find, just like you found some on your way up.

That I can relate with. Why do you think that I am sharing so much wisdom in my books? Because I do not dare to melt everything away once I have completed the journey. They might be outdated and old to me, but we shared such a history.

Writing, I cleaned up and polished them so there are ready for you. Writing, I also have the chance to relive our history once more, before parting ways. It is my way to say farewell to what I am leaving behind.

This works well with mindset, tools, and ideas. It is not the same with people. Once we have awoken, we must cocoon and rise. To hang around in our old neighborhoods will be the best way to hurt or to be hurt.

You will hurt those you love as you are trying to show them the light that you've just found. You will burn them and traumatize them with and from your love, trying to liberate them. So don't bother, if you love them, you have to let them be, until they are ready.

Now that we solve that problem of hurting those we love, what is the purpose of hanging around any longer? Those surrounding you, those who knew who you were since the beginning of your evolution at the base of the pyramid, will never accept that you have changed, even less, accept your rise.

And this is how jealousy will be showing its ugly face, using people you know on a first-name basis. Not all of them will be affected by jealousy, but the majority will. It is not because there were bad people, it just the change of dynamic that propel both of you on another path.

See it like this. You are changing. You are rising. There are not. How do you think that they are feeling? They will never accept that you understood something that they haven't, so you must be cheating. What to you was a personal quest, looking for your wings and purpose, to them, it is a reminder that they are stuck at the glass ceiling and haven't made peace with themselves yet.

In other words, because they are not ready to cocoon, they hate you because you did and you are now better. They will point out what you left behind, they will use guilt to reattach your anchors... misery loves company.

Is that jealousy? Jealousy is to want something that you do not possess. I tried that hypothesis lately. I am rising. I have honors and achievements causing the jealousy coming with my presence.

Well, lately, I opened those up to people that could be jealous. You know what? They turned them down. I was mesmerized for a little while since my understanding of jealousy was so far off.

This was not jealousy, but a complex. They hate you that much because you reminded them of the inner voice they are trying to silence and to keep in check. It is not about you, but not at all. It was their internal fight that they are suffering from. You were just the recipient of the hatred.

So how do I deal with jealousy nowadays? I keep an open mind and heart and I smile. What I know and learn on the way, I shared those in my books, for them, for all of you, once you are ready. But understanding the reality of the dynamic, I realized how important it was to not get attached, ever.

Wasn't it in the Bible that if you look back, you will turn into a status of salt? Our forefathers and foremothers understood the concept and really tried to transmit its wisdom. The message got lost in translation somehow… and the worse thing is there was no translation needed, the imagery was clear and straight forward, only the context needed to be clarified.

> "No attachment, no hurt."
> Dr. Bak Nguyen

And do I keep giving? Of course, I keep giving without any expectation in return. I give because at the giving end is where the growth happens. Was that selfless or selfish? I do not care much about the label, not anymore.

It is the same action. The result will be evaluated by the receiving end, if people are ready and open, they will appreciate. If they were not ready, they still feel the vibe of change and will hate you to have reminded them of their suffering and indecision.

In the lack of a better word, we call that jealousy. But jealousy it is not. It is about being ready and comfortable with who we are. On that, we started this journey by saying that to reinvent yourself isn't about change, but to reveal who you were really inside. That was the only justification that could urge such strong feelings.

It is the same with jealousy. The hate is not from wanting what you have, it is from the knowledge that you have something that they might never have. Even if you offer it, they know that they might not be ready… and from that, hate is flourishing.

I gave you my reasoning, but if you want more, I found a way to leverage that certitude of jealousy and to surf its energy, because, make no mistake, hate is a very powerful energy.

Well, the only way I found to beat jealousy at its own game was to be faster than its understanding. I used the social networks to announce, in advance, my challenge and leverage the judgment and the hatred to keep myself accountable. By doing so, I defeat procrastination, completely.

Then, to combat jealousy, I need to set my achievement faster than people could realize what I just did. If they are a step behind, jealousy is unavoidable. If I am 3 steps ahead, well, they don't even bother to compare anymore. They just don't like me, but it wasn't about me, now they know that it is about them.

So this is the simple strategy that I used to combat effectively jealousy and to surf the powerful waves of hate, by accelerating. Well, if today I am known around the world, it is thanks to my speed and momentum. Where do you think that came from? It was me leveraging hate!

For those of you intrigued with the power of momentum and speed, I wrote 2 books on the matter: **MOMENTUM TRANSFER**, co-written with coach Dino Masson and **TORNADO**. Those two books breakdown the art and secret of creating and riding momentums.

In this journey, just know that you did not have to put up with such negativity. Know that there is a way to leverage that energy and to rise, higher and faster thanks to it. And hate? Well, eventually, they will understand and walk their own path. Eventually.

This is **1SELF,** reinvent yourself from any crisis.

To be faster than EVOLUTION,
To keep our RELEVANCY and FUN
Thanks to CONFIDENCE,
HUMILITY and INNOCENCE,

That's the journey ahead.
That's the promise of **1SELF**.

Dr. BAK NGUYEN

CONCLUSION
by Dr. BAK NGUYEN

I have a hard time accepting that this is already the end of this journey. It seems that we are just beginning. Well, this is the magic of reinventing ourselves; we, somehow, escape the grasp of time.

Once calm and harmonious with yourself, once whole, you will see that everything is moving slowly, moving peacefully all around you. And all that you are doing is reacting. That's your perspective, from the center of change. For the others looking at us from the outside, well, we moved so fast and covered so much ground.

The only way for them to explain our achievements and their pace was that we were cheating… This is an interesting way to see it. Let indulge them with their perspectives.

From our end, the secret was because we are not whole, reunited with our inner voice and freed from the burden of emotions, lies, and peer pressures. We move faster because there is nothing anchoring us down. Them, they have their values and attachments, all of them.

On that matter, it is the subject of an entire book, but I would like to surf it with you before the end of this journey. How can one generate more energy? Here's another gift to you to celebrate your rise:

$$\text{ENERGY} \propto \frac{\text{WILL} \cdot \text{DESIRE}}{\text{VALUES}}$$

Well, I wrote a whole book, **THE ENERGY FORMULA** covering in-depth that matter. The main logic is that our values are what's dividing our available energy. Well, in the cocoon, what did we do? We melt those values into new ones.

Before the new ones are settling in, make sure that those are the values you hold dear, because to each value you a holding, there is a price attached with it.

That also explains how we advanced so quickly, while we were melting our values and identity, we had more energy available. I told you to find your **WHY**. That was your desire. And your **WILL**, that was what awoke you in the first place.

Can you feel the perfect storm rising in your favor? The rise in energy is simply intoxicating. And that energy will liberate at your first win, and at the second, and the following ones. I just revisited the whole journey within simple lines.

And with the energy formula, you now have a better understanding of how the magic works, behind the curtains.

In the introduction, we talked about **balance**, **confidence**, **humility**, and **innocence**. Well, the **balance**, we covered as you are melting away your values and goal in the cocoon. What you let go and melted, you won't have to balance anymore.

The **confidence**, we addressed that aiming for your first win and building your new self from the product of each step ahead, wins, and losses.

Humility? We covered that also as you are finding a WHY based on your love for someone else. That does not only keep you humble, it keeps you confident and dedicated.

And **innocence**? Well, innocence is the ability to relive again and again the same events with the joy and magic of the first time. I told you to keep an open heart and an open mind to keep nourishing your journey and your growth. Embrace innocence and being open just get much easier.

On the way, doubts and pride were your demons. Those are all coming with your attachments to the past, people, wins, losses, scars, and love. Don't deny yourself the moment to feel, feel it completely, and let go.

Make yourself available to live the next feeling, as fully as the last one. If you are doing so, every time, your energy will go through the roof from your desire and will. And as you let go, your values are now not getting any heavier… please picture the energy formula clearly.

You have now awoken. You are out of your cocoon and your rise is for you to live and to enjoy. Rising is about energy and feeling, not a direction. This also means that you are free to decide where to go. Even better, you can change your mind as often as you want.

> "If you are more than you have, changing direction to adapt to the flow of life should not be that big of a challenge."
> Dr. Bak Nguyen

And who has much will fear. Who is much is simply confident. And you all know that by now. If you followed my journey, this is my favorite quote. A great one, and one holding much truth and power to those you can understand its meaning, not the bragging.

> "Confidence is sexy."
> Dr. Bak Nguyen

So to reinvent ourselves does not mean to restart at the bottom of the pyramid every time. It means to cross the glass ceiling and to rise above the animal instincts, the primal needs.

To reinvent yourself also means to have the courage to make a stand to allow yourself to finally shine. You are doing so because it was always meant to be, for your essence and life force to be expressed and released.

To reinvent yourself has at its core the component of humility since you know that you must readjust. Only before, you were readjusting being the same, holding the same principles and values. How can you change staying the same? Now, you have your cocoon to melt your values, goal, and identity and to emerge new, better, lighter.

And to reinvent yourself holds the magic that will keep the journey coming, the fun and surprise element. Keep the heart of a child, of innocence to enjoy every minute of the ride. With an open heart, it is fun. With an open mind, it will teach you much more and much faster. Oh, and must I add, without much scars.

Rise and have fun. Spread your wings, reinvent your wings, find new wings, the choice is yours. And you can try them all. Just like love can be multiplied, love and you will hold its power. Love without attachment. Otherwise, you are playing the game of Attention.

Love, embrace and reinvent. This is **1SELF,** reinvent yourself from any crisis.

This is **1SELF,** reinvent yourself from any crisis.

To be faster than EVOLUTION,
To keep our RELEVANCY and FUN
Thanks to CONFIDENCE,
HUMILITY and INNOCENCE,

That's the journey ahead.
That's the promise of **1SELF**.

Dr. BAK NGUYEN

ABOUT THE AUTHOR

From Canada, **Dr. BAK NGUYEN**, Nominee Ernst and Young Entrepreneur of the year, Grand Homage Lys DIVERSITY, LinkedIn & TownHall Achiever of the year and TOP 100 Doctors 2021. Dr Bak is a cosmetic dentist, CEO and founder of Mdex & Co. His company is revolutionizing the dental field. Speaker and motivator, he wrote 72 books over 36 months accumulating many world records (to be officialized). His books are covering:

- **ENTREPRENEURSHIP**
- **LEADERSHIP**
- **QUEST OF IDENTITY**
- **DENTISTRY AND MEDICINE**
- **PARENTING**
- **CHILDREN BOOKS**
- **PHILOSOPHY**

In 2003, he founded Mdex, a dental company upon which in 2018, he launched the most ambitious private endeavour to reform the dental industry, Canada wide. Philosopher, he has close to his heart the quest of happiness of the people surrounding him, patients and colleagues alike. In 2020, he launched an International collaborative initiative named **THE ALPHAS** to share knowledge and for Entrepreneurs and Doctors to thrive through the Greatest Pandemic and Economic depression of our time.

In 2016, he co-found with Tranie Vo, Emotive World Incorporated, a tech research company to use technology to empower happiness and sharing. U.A.X. the ultimate audio experience is the landmark project on which the team is advancing, utilizing the technics of the movie industry and the advancement in ARTIFICIAL INTELLIGENCE to save the book industry and to upgrade the continuing education space.

These projects have allowed Dr Nguyen to attract interests from the international and diplomatic community and he is now the center of a global discussion in the wellbeing and the future of the health profession. It is in that matter that he shares his thoughts and encourages the health community to share their own stories.

"It's not worth it go through it alone! Together, we stand, alone, we fall."

Motivational speaker and serial entrepreneur, philosopher and author, from his own words, Dr Nguyen describes himself as a dentist by circumstances, an entrepreneur by nature and a communicator by passion.

He also holds recognitions from the Canadian Parliament and the Canadian Senate.

www.DrBakNguyen.com

AMAZON - BARNES & NOBLE - APPLE BOOKS - KINDLE
SPOTIFY - APPLE MUSIC

ULTIMATE AUDIO EXPERIENCE

A new way to learn and enjoy Audiobooks. Made to be entertaining while keeping the self-educational value of a book, UAX will appeal to both auditive and visual people. UAX is the blockbuster of the Audiobooks.

UAX will cover most of Dr Bak's books, and is now negotiating to bring more authors and more titles to the UAX concept. Now streaming on Spotify, Apple Music and available for download on all major music platforms. Give it a try today!

AMAZON - BARNES & NOBLE - APPLE BOOKS - KINDLE
SPOTIFY - APPLE MUSIC

COMBO
PAPERBACK/AUDIOBOOK
ACTIVATION

Please register your book to receive the link to your audiobook version. Register at: https://baknguyen.com/1self-registry

Your license of the audiobook allows you to share with up to 3 peoples the audiobook contained at this link. Book published by Dr. Bak publishing company. Audiobook produced by Emotive World Inc. Copyright 2021, All right reserved.

FROM THE SAME AUTHOR
Dr Bak Nguyen

www.DrBakNguyen.com

FACTEUR HUMAIN 032
LE LEADERSHIP DU SUCCÈS
par Dr. BAK NGUYEN & CHRISTIAN TRUDEAU

002 **La Symphonie des Sens**
ENTREPREUNARIAT
par Dr. BAK NGUYEN

ehappyPedia 037
THE RISE OF THE UNICORN
BY Dr. BAK NGUYEN & Dr. JEAN DE SERRES

006 **Industries Disruptors**
BY Dr .BAK NGUYEN

007 **Changing the World from a dental chair**
BY Dr. BAK NGUYEN

CHAMPION MINDSET 038
LEARNING TO WIN
BY Dr. BAK NGUYEN & CHRISTOPHE MULUMBA

008 **The Power Behind the Alpha**
BY TRANIE VO & Dr. BAK NGUYEN

BRANDING DrBAK 039
BALANCING STRATEGY AND EMOTIONS
BY Dr. BAK NGUYEN

035 **SELFMADE**
GRATITUDE AND HUMILITY
BY Dr. BAK NGUYEN

THE RISE OF THE UNICORN 2 076
eHappyPedia
BY Dr BAK NGUYEN & Dr JEAN DE SERRES

072 **THE U.A.X. STORY**
THE ULTIMATE AUDIO EXPERIENCE
BY Dr. BAK NGUYEN

SYMPHONY OF SKILLS 001
BY Dr. BAK NGUYEN

CHILDREN'S BOOK
with William Bak

The Trilogy of Legends

THE LEGEND OF THE CHICKEN HEART 016
LA LÉGENDE DU COEUR DE POULET 017
BY Dr. BAK NGUYEN & WILLIAM BAK

THE LEGEND OF THE LION HEART 018
LA LÉGENDE DU COEUR DE LION 019
BY Dr. BAK NGUYEN & WILLIAM BAK

THE LEGEND OF THE DRAGON HEART 020
LA LÉGENDE DU COEUR DE DRAGON 021
BY Dr. BAK NGUYEN & WILLIAM BAK

WE ARE ALL DRAGONS 022
NOUS TOUS, DRAGONS 023
BY Dr. BAK NGUYEN & WILLIAM BAK

THE 9 SECRETS OF THE SMART CHICKEN 025
LES 9 SECRETS DU POULET INTELLIGENT 026
BY Dr. BAK NGUYEN & WILLIAM BAK

THE SECRET OF THE FAST CHICKEN 027
LE SECRETS DU POULET RAPIDE 028
BY Dr. BAK NGUYEN & WILLIAM BAK

THE LEGEND OF THE SUPER CHICKEN 029
LA LÉGENDE DU SUPER POULET 030
BY Dr. BAK NGUYEN & WILLIAM BAK

031 **THE STORY OF THE CHICKEN SHIT**
032 **L'HISTOIRE DU CACA DE POULET**
BY Dr. BAK NGUYEN & WILLIAM BAK

033 **WHY CHICKEN CAN'T DREAM?**
034 **POURQUOI LES POULETS NE RÊVENT PAS?**
BY Dr. BAK NGUYEN & WILLIAM BAK

057 **THE STORY OF THE CHICKEN NUGGET**
BY Dr. BAK NGUYEN & WILLIAM BAK

THE SPIES AND ALIENS COLLECTION

077 **THE VACCINE**
079 **LE VACCIN**
077B **LA VACUNA**
BY Dr BAK NGUYEN & WILLIAM BAK
TRANSLATION BY BRENDA GARCIA

DENTISTRY

PROFESSION HEALTH - TOME ONE 005
THE UNCONVENTIONAL
QUEST OF HAPPINESS
BY Dr. BAK NGUYEN, Dr. MIRJANA SINDOLIC,
Dr. ROBERT DURAND AND COLLABORATORS

HOW TO NOT FAIL AS A DENTIST 046
BY Dr. BAK NGUYEN

SUCCESS IS A CHOICE 060
BLUEPRINTS FOR HEALTH
PROFESSIONALS
BY Dr. BAK NGUYEN

RELEVANCY - TOME TWO 064
REINVENTING OURSELVES TO SURVIVE
BY Dr. BAK NGUYEN & Dr. PAUL OUELLETTE AND
COLLABORATORS

MIDAS TOUCH 065
POST-COVID DENTISTRY
BY Dr. BAK NGUYEN, Dr. JULIO REYNAFARJE AND
Dr. PAUL OUELLETTE

THE POWER OF DR 066
THE MODERN TITLE OF NOBILITY
BY Dr. BAK NGUYEN, Dr. PAVEL KRASTEV AND
COLLABORATORS

QUEST OF IDENTITY

004 **IDENTITY**
THE ANTHOLOGY OF QUESTS
BY Dr. BAK NGUYEN

011 **HYBRID**
THE MODERN QUEST OF IDENTITY
BY Dr. BAK NGUYEN

015 **FORCES OF NATURE**
FORGING THE CHARACTER
OF WINNERS
BY Dr. BAK NGUYEN

LIFESTYLE

045 **HORIZON, BUILDING UP THE VISION**
VOLUME ONE
BY Dr. BAK NGUYEN

047- **HORIZON, ON THE FOOTSTEPS
OF TITANS**
VOLUME TWO
BY Dr. BAK NGUYEN

068- **HORIZON, DREAMING OF TRAVELING**
VOLUME THREE
BY Dr. BAK NGUYEN

MILLION DOLLAR MINDSET

MOMENTUM TRANSFER 009
BY Dr. BAK NGUYEN & Coach DINO MASSON

LEVERAGE 014
COMMUNICATION INTO SUCCESS
BY Dr. BAK NGUYEN AND COLLABORATORS

HOW TO WRITE A BOOK IN 30 DAYS 040
BY Dr. BAK NGUYEN

POWER 042
EMOTIONAL INTELLIGENCE
BY Dr. BAK NGUYEN

HOW TO WRITE A SUCCESSFUL BUSINESS PLAN 048
BY Dr BAK NGUYEN & ROUBA SAKR

MINDSET ARMORY 049
BY Dr. BAK NGUYEN

MASTERMIND, 7 WAYS INTO THE BIG LEAGUE 052
BY Dr. BAK NGUYEN & JONAS DIOP

PLAYBOOK INTRODUCTION 055
BY Dr. BAK NGUYEN

PLAYBOOK INTRODUCTION 2 056
BY Dr. BAK NGUYEN

062 **RISING**
TO WIN MORE THAN YOU ARE AFRAID TO LOSE
BY Dr. BAK NGUYEN

067 **TORNADO**
FORCE OF CHANGE
BY Dr. BAK NGUYEN

071 **BOOTCAMP**
BOOKS TO REWRITE MINDSETS INTO WINNING STATES OF MIND
BY Dr. BAK NGUYEN

PARENTING

024 **THE BOOK OF LEGENDS**
BY Dr. BAK NGUYEN & WILLIAM BAK

041 **THE BOOK OF LEGENDS 2**
BY Dr. BAK NGUYEN & WILLIAM BAK

051 **THE BOOK OF LEGENDS 3**
THE END OF THE INNOCENCE AGE
BY Dr. BAK NGUYEN & WILLIAM BAK

PERSONAL GROWTH

REBOOT 012
MIDLIFE CRISIS
BY Dr. BAK NGUYEN

HUMILITY FOR SUCCESS 050
BALANCING STRATEGY AND EMOTIONS
BY Dr. BAK NGUYEN

THE ENERGY FORMULA 053
BY Dr. BAK NGUYEN

AMONGST THE ALPHA 058
BY Dr. BAK NGUYEN & COLLABORATORS

AMONGST THE ALPHA vol.2 059
ON THE OTHER SIDE
BY Dr. BAK NGUYEN & COLLABORATORS

THE 90 DAYS CHALLENGE 061
BY Dr. BAK NGUYEN

EMPOWERMENT 069
BY Dr BAK NGUYEN

THE MODERN WOMAN 070
TO HAVE IT HAVE WITH NO SACRIFICE
BY Dr. BAK NGUYEN & Dr. EMILY LETRAN

ALPHA LADDERS 075
CAPTAIN OF YOUR DESTINY
BY Dr BAK NGUYEN & JONAS DIOP

PHILOSOPHY

003 **LEADERSHIP**
PANDORA'S BOX
BY Dr. BAK NGUYEN

043 **KRYPTO**
TO SAVE THE WORLD
BY Dr. BAK NGUYEN & ILYAS BAKOUCH

SOCIETY

013 **LE RÊVE CANADIEN**
D'IMMIGRANT À MILLIONNAIRE
par DR BAK NGUYEN

054 **CHOC**
LE JARDIN D'EDITH
par DR BAK NGUYEN

063 **AFTERMATH**
BUSINESS AFTER THE GREAT PAUSE
BY Dr BAK NGUYEN & Dr ERIC LACOSTE

073 **TOUCHSTONE**
LEVERAGING TODAY'S P
SYCHOLOGICAL SMOG
BY Dr BAK NGUYEN & Dr KEN SEROTA

074 **COVIDCONOMICS**
THE GENERATION AHEAD
BY Dr BAK NGUYEN & COLLABORATORS

ALPHA LADDERS 2 081
SHAPING LEADERS AND ACHIEVERS
BY Dr BAK NGUYEN & BRENDA GARCIA

THE POWER OF YES 010
VOLUME ONE: IMPACT
BY Dr BAK NGUYEN

THE POWER OF YES 2 036
VOLUME TWO: SHAPELESS
BY Dr BAK NGUYEN

THE POWER OF YES 3 039
VOLUME THREE: LIMITLESS
BY Dr BAK NGUYEN

THE POWER OF YES 4 082
VOLUME FOUR: PURPOSE
BY Dr BAK NGUYEN

THE POWER OF YES 5 083
VOLUME FIVE: ALPHA
BY Dr BAK NGUYEN

THE POWER OF YES 6 084
VOLUME SIX: PERSPECTIVE
BY Dr BAK NGUYEN

TITLES AVAILABLE AT
www.DrBakNguyen.com

AMAZON - BARNES & NOBLE - APPLE BOOKS - KINDLE
SPOTIFY - APPLE MUSIC

TITLES AVAILABLE AT
www.DrBakNguyen.com

AMAZON - BARNES & NOBLE - APPLE BOOKS - KINDLE
SPOTIFY - APPLE MUSIC

www.ingramcontent.com/pod-product-compliance
Lightning Source LLC
Chambersburg PA
CBHW071511150426
43191CB00009B/1489